Contents

1	Crisis!	4	18	The Post Office and Railways	38
2	The Mail Goes Through	6	19	The Great Train Robbery	40
3	The Post Office Organization	8	20	The Post Office Railway	42
4	Behind the Counter	10	21	Other Transport	44
5	Sorting	12	22	Designing Postage Stamps	46
6	'Bag Time, Gentlemen!'	14	23	Producing the Stamps	48
7	The Postman's Walk	16	24	Stamp Collecting	50
8	Out and About	18	25	British Telecom	52
9	The Sub-Post Office	20	26	The Post Office Tower	54
10	Joining the Post Office	22	27	The Future	56
11	Parcel Post	24			
12	Save it!	26		Facts and Figures	58
13	Finance	28		Important Dates and Events	61
14	The First Postal Service	30		Glossary	62
15	The Postal Services Develop	32		Further Reading	62
16	A Postal Service for All	34		Index	63
17	In the Mail	36			

1 Crisis!

It is five o'clock in the morning. Most people are still in bed. In the sorting department attached to the post office men and women have been at work for some time.

Sorting all the mail requires concentration, as this picture shows.

Mailbags have been collected from the early trains arriving at the local railway station. They have been loaded into vans and brought to the sorting office.

One of the sorters is checking through the pile of packages on the table before him. Some of them have come a long way from the box where they were posted. Letters and parcels are frequently handled by as many as eleven different people between being posted and being delivered.

Suddenly the sorter stops. he looks again at a small parcel before him. Something about it makes him uneasy. It is addressed to the town's Member of Parliament.

The sorter comes to a decision. He calls over a supervisor and indicates the parcel. The other man studies it intently . Then he glances at the sorter.

'You think it's a letter bomb, don't you?' he asks quietly.

The sorter shrugs his shoulders. 'I don't know,' he confesses. 'It's just a feeling I've got. That package is the same shape and size as the one they found in London last week. And look who it's addressed to.'

'I know, that's what worries me,' says the supervisor. 'M.P.s get all sorts of crank letters. All the same . . .' He thinks for a moment and then nods decisively. 'All right, I'm not taking any chances. I'm going to treat it as a bomb. You know the drill.'

This is a signal for controlled activity in the building. Quietly the area around the sorting racks is cleared of all personnel.

Two sorters check the receipts for registered mail to see that everything is in order.

The supervisor knows that there is a great deal to be done. Telephone calls will have to be made to the police and to the head postmaster, telling them what has happened. The fire brigade will be called, and the police may ask the army to send a bomb-disposal squad.

The supervisor shakes his head. He is glad that working for the Post Office is not always as exciting and nerve-racking as this.

There are 48 pigeonholes in each frame, each one for a different road on a 'walk'.

② The Mail Goes Through

People line up at the post office's counter for stamps and postal orders. Parcels are weighed, receipts given and licences bought. It is a busy but normal high street scene; one that is being repeated in towns and cities all over the country.

Yet some of the most exciting stories in the history of the world are connected with the carrying of messages. For thousands of years men and women have tried to obey the instruction: 'the mail must go through'. In doing so many of them have risked and even lost their lives.

In North Africa messengers have urged their frightened camels through sandstorms and across vast deserts. Pony Express riders have fought off Red Indians as they raced their exhausted mounts across the prairies of the U.S.A. Intrepid pilots have nursed their tiny, single-engined aircraft across the towering mountain ranges of South America. Runners have loped through African jungles or swum across crocodile-infested rivers. All of them had one aim in mind – to deliver the mail with which they had been entrusted.

Many post officers have a queuing system to speed things up during busy periods.

Will my letter get there in time? A customer checks the timetable in a post office.

All too often the work of the Post Office is not appreciated and its difficulties are not fully understood. Behind the post office in the high street is a huge, complicated organization employing thousands of people. From designing stamps to controlling a special underground railways system, from loading aircraft to delivering postcards, the Post Office's workers know that the main aim of the service is the same as it was thousands of years ago in Persia or ancient Greece — 'the mail must go through'.

A great deal of administrative work goes on behind the scenes at any post office.

Today it is customary to sneer at the postal service, to complain because letters are late in arriving or because there are long queues and slow service at some post offices.

Up and down the country, however, in spite of many difficulties the post offices do serve the public. Most of their employees are hard-working and dedicated to their task of delivering the mail.

Letters reach their destinations in spite of terrible weather conditions. Parcels are sorted even when there is a risk of a maniac planting a bomb in one of them. Post offices and postal vans have been held up and robbed and workers viciously attacked. Trains carrying mail have been stopped and ransacked. Aircraft taking airmail across the country have crashed.

3 The Post Office Organization

Behind the post offices in our high streets is an enormous organization employing over 170,000 people.

For a hundred years the Post Office was responsible for both the delivery of mail and for the national telephone system. Now, however, the telephone service is managed by British Telecom.

The main task of the Post Office is to collect and distribute mail up and down the country. Some 122,500 men and women do this. They include postmen, sorters, mechanics, technicians and administrators.

In the year 1978–79, the mail carriers handled over 9,337 million letters and 160 million parcels. Collections were made from 100,000 post boxes and mail delivered to 22 million addresses.

The great problem facing the organizers is that in Britain people expect their mail to be delivered by breakfast time, and eighty-six per cent of it does arrive by 9.30 a.m.

However, this means that most of the people involved in delivering the mail have to work at the same time, early in the morning. If mail deliveries could be staggered over the whole day it would be more efficient, but unpopular.

Another 36,000 employees work in the high street post offices, including counter staff and administrators. There are more than 22,500 post offices in the country, 1,600 of which are run by Post Office staff, the other by sub-postmasters.

Under the direction of a head postmaster, responsible for all the postal services in the area, the counter staff have to deal with all the varied activities which take place in a post office.

Pensions, unemployment benefits and family allowances are paid out. Licences are issued for dogs, motor cars and television sets. Stamps and postal orders are sold, parcels weighed and a

---

The Post Office is called a labour-intensive industry because it employs a lot of people.

number of savings schemes operated. Every ten minutes in Britain over a million pounds changes hands over post office counters.

The Post Office also operates the National Girobank service. An account may be opened at any post office with a deposit of £10. The service operates from an office near Liverpool.

The Data Processing Service administered by the Post Office uses computers scattered all over the country. A business organization may pay to have these computers solve a financial or administrative problem.

Counter staff in our high street post offices have a demanding and varied job to do.

The long queues in this post office show how much we need the services of the Post Office.

4 Behind the Counter

Most high street post offices are open from 9.00 a.m. until 5.30 p.m. for five days a week; and from 9.00 a.m. until 12.30 or 1.00 p.m. on Saturdays. An exception to this is the famous Trafalgar Square branch in London, which is open from 8.00 a.m. until 8.00 p.m. every day except Christmas Day.

By the time the post office doors open for business, the counter assistants will have been at work for some time, getting their positions ready.

When the first customers come in a counter assistant never knows what she might be asked for. What she has to remember is that, for many people, a visit to a post office, unlike entering other shops, may be quite a nerve-racking experience.

'We may get an old person worried about her pension, or someone wanting to send an urgent telegram,' explained one assistant. 'They'll be under strain. We have to remember that when we deal with them.'

The counter assistant will be asked all sorts of questions. Those dealing with letter-post are usually the easiest to answer. There is the two-tier system of first- and second-class mail, with almost ninety-three per cent of the former arriving the day after it has been posted.

If someone wants proof of delivery, there is the special service known as recorded delivery, where the postman receives a receipt when he hands the letter over. The special delivery service ensures that a letter is sent to its destination even if it arrives too late for the usual postal round.

There are some areas in which the Post Office service is up against competition. More people now have bank accounts and cheque books, so there is less demand for postal orders than once

Helping customers to fill in forms is just one of the many duties of counter staff.

Counter staff have to be prepared to serve at any window during the day's work.

was the case. In the same way, with more people owning telephones, fewer telegrams are being sent from post offices. Even so, about 150 million telegrams are still dispatched every year by telephone or carrier.

One of the major responsibilities of a counter assistant is to help pay out pensions upon the production of a pension book. Among the pensions regularly paid out in post offices are Widows', Retirement and War Benefit, Child Benefit, and Family Income Supplement.

A member of the staff training team helps a counter assistant to learn her job.

5 Sorting

Letters and packages are being collected from Britain's 100,000 postboxes continually during the day. The postmen take them back to the post offices' sorting office.

The average sorting office may start work as early as four in the morning. The sorters have two main tasks. One is to sort the incoming mail intended for addresses in their region. The second is to sort the letters and parcels collected locally and intended for destinations outside the area. These are put into sacks according to region and dispatched by road or rail.

In the larger post offices there are full-time sorters who do nothing but allocate the mail. In the smaller offices the postmen sort all the mail before they go out on their rounds.

The larger establishments use machines to help them cope with the volume of work. All the mail is put into a large revolving drum, called a segregator. Packages go straight through the drum to be sorted by hand; letters are shaken out through slots to a conveyor belt.

The letters are then placed in piles on another machine called the automatic letter facer, or ALF for short. ALF turns the envelopes round so that the stamps are on top, separates them into first- and second-class mail, and then cancels the stamps, defacing them so that they cannot be used again.

Next the letters go to the letter-coding desks. They pass before operators sitting at coding machines. The operators read the postcode on the addresses and copy it on their machines. This transfers the code in dots on to the envelopes.

Finally the automatic letter-sorting machine scans the pattern of dots on the envelopes and feeds them into the appropriate sections for delivery by the postmen.

In sorting offices without machines, the sorting

Sacks of incoming mail are emptied before the work of sorting can begin.

A sorter fills the sacks of outgoing mail. Each has its destination clearly labelled.

is done by hand. Sorters sit before frames divided into sections. Each section bears on it the name of a county or large town, and there are forty-eight sections to each frame. The letters are placed on a frame before the sorter and he flicks them into the right pigeonholes in front of him.

These men put codes on to letters so that they can be sorted easily by machine.

'Bag Time, Gentlemen'

The sorting department of any post office is a busy and bustling place. There is a great deal to do and not a great deal of time in which to do it.

Sorters have to work to a series of deadlines which must be met. Mail must go out with the postmen at stated times, or reach railway stations in time to be loaded on to trains.

When the mail has been sorted into the forty-eight pigeonholes on a rack, it is taken into another corner of the sorting office where it is sub-divided still further and then placed into sacks for transportation to post offices in other towns and villages.

After the parcels have been sorted and placed into sacks, they are sent down chutes to loading bays below. Here a van will be waiting with a postman. He loads the sacks into the van and sets off.

In another corner of the sorting office there will be an office with large glass windows. Locked inside this office senior sorters will be going

Parcels come down chutes to the sorting office. Mail arrives throughout the day.

through the registered mail, checking it and entering it in a book. When they have gone through all the registered packages, they will distribute them to the postmen to deliver.

New postmen will be working at a variety of jobs in the sorting office. They are usually given thirteen weeks' training, which includes a session in the sorting department. In addition to assisting with the sorting, they may be asked to operate the date stamp. All local mail will have a postmark stamped on it in the sorting office, showing when it was collected.

From four until six in the morning everyone will be particularly busy, with a backlog of mail delivered earlier to be sorted. From time to time the inspector in charge of the office will call out 'Bag time, gentlemen!' At this the sorters will assemble to put parcels and letters into the sacks from the piles already sorted and packaged. The bags will be sealed with clips and taken out or sent down the chute to the waiting vans.

Registered mail is kept in a special office and must be signed for by a postman.

In larger post offices parcels are sorted with the aid of computers and closed-circuit TVs.

7 The Postman's Walk

The postman's day may start as early as 4.30 a.m. Many find it difficult to get up while it is still dark. 'It's bad enough in summer,' said one, 'but in the winter it can be really dreadful.'

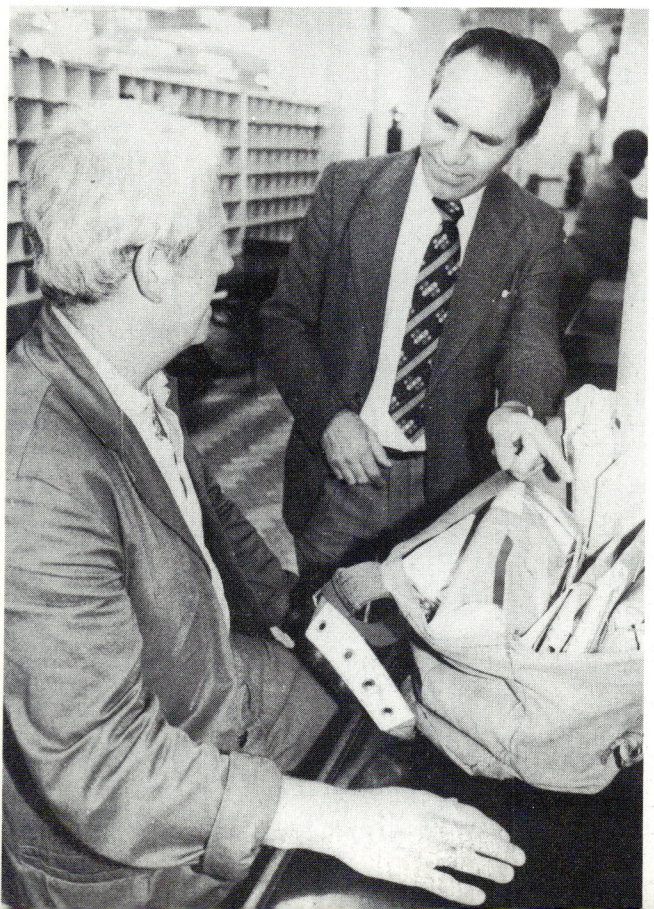

A supervisor talks to a postman who has finished sorting the mail for his 'walk'.

Wearing the postman's dark grey suit with scarlet edging — or if it is summer a light grey suit — he will report for duty at the sorting office. Even this early in the morning some people are cheerful and noisy, but the majority of postmen come in quietly.

The bright lights of the sorting office contrast with the dark streets outside. The postman will probably find that sorters or postmen on the night shift have already piled up the letters for his area.

He takes the piles over to his rack and starts to sort them out. Using elastic bands or lengths of string, he ties the letters into bundles according to the different roads and streets on his 'walk', as it is known.

The postman will try to arrange the letters so that he can deliver those intended for one side of the street first, and then cross over to the other side.

He will be so busy that he will hardly notice that the office is gradually coming to life and that the hum of conversation is becoming a roar as postmen exchange letters and help each other make out illegible addresses. 'We're not supposed to deliver a letter unless it's correctly addressed,' said one postman, 'but we do our best to find out where all the mail should be going, so that we don't disappoint anyone.'

Set high in one of the walls are several windows with smoked glass in them, so that no one from the sorting office can see through them. The postmen know, however, that standing behind these windows there may be supervisors or executives, watching the sorting office to make sure that nothing dishonest goes on below. 'We don't like being spied on,' said a postman, 'but it has to be done. A lot of valuable packages come through the sorting office.'

Reporting for duty! This postman is signing in before beginning his day's work.

When the postman has finished sorting, he may have time for a quick cup of tea in the canteen. Then, at about 7 a.m., it will be time to set out on his walk.

There is always time for a bite to eat in the canteen between jobs!

⑧ Out and About

The postman may make his rounds on foot or on one of the 70,000 bicycles owned by the Post Office. For larger areas or heavy loads, he may drive one of the official red vans with the inscription EIIR on the side. These are maintained by mechanics in the post office's garages.

The Post Office has its own mechanics to service its vehicles and keep them roadworthy.

Carrying his sack or pushing a trolley before him, the postman will be a familiar and often a welcome figure on his walk, especially to the housebound or elderly. The Post Office authorities appreciate that the postman is their main link with the public.

'We do what we can to help,' said a postman. 'If there's some elderly person on our route and we don't see her for several days, we might knock at the door just to see that she's all right.'

Above all, the postman hopes for good weather on his route. Five hundred years before the birth of Christ, it was written of the Persian postal messengers that 'neither rain nor snow prevented them from carrying out their appointed task'. A great New York post office has these words engraved over its doors.

All the same, the postman would prefer to

The mail comes down a chute from the sorting office to be loaded into a van.

The Post Office uses a variety of vehicles. These mopeds are used to deliver telegrams.

make his rounds in the dry. 'There are enough nuisances in good weather,' one said. 'When it's raining as well it all gets a bit much.'

Most postmen have their own pet hates. Snapping dogs, spitting cats, slippery roads and inaccessible letter boxes come high on the list of most of them.

The modern postman also has a number of other duties. He may have to collect the posted mail from postboxes on his walk. He uses a special key collected at the post office for this. He will also alter the small panel on the box showing the time of the next collection, taking the new tab from inside the box.

Among his packages there may be registered items and recorded-delivery letters which must be signed for. He will also deliver cash-on-delivery parcels, collecting the money and giving a receipt.

The postman hopes that there are not too many receipts for his walk, because getting people out of bed can be time-consuming.

9 The Sub-Post Office

Almost 21,000 post offices in Britain are not manned by full-time Post Office staff. These are the small sub-post offices to be found in towns and villages everywhere.

A sub-post office is a shop, often a general store. A corner of it is given over to Post Office business. The sub-postmaster sells stamps and postal orders, pays out pensions, issues licences and weighs parcels, just like his colleagues in the large post offices.

The Post Office gives an agency for a sub-post office wherever it thinks that one is needed, and where there is no other post office in the vicinity.

The sub-postmaster is paid a salary from the Post Office in return for his services. He also

A typical sub-post office. This chemist's shop has a special section for Post Office business.

Most of the facilities of a large post office can be found in a sub-post office.

keeps the profits from the rest of his shop.

If an agency becomes vacant in a district, the Post Office must advertise it for three weeks. Anyone may apply for the position. As a rule the person who is buying the store containing the sub-post office has a good chance of receiving the agency, but this does not always happen. 'It's nerve-racking while you're waiting to hear,' said one sub-postmistress. 'You need the post office side to subsidize the rest of the shop.'

Applicants for the agency will be interviewed by Post Office officials. The successful candidate will have to convince the executives that he or she is of good character, has a sense of business and that the premises to house the post office are safe and secure.

The successful applicant will be sent on a course by the Post Office. Here he or she will learn all that is necessary to be a good counter clerk. 'It's a very crammed course,' said a sub-postmaster, 'but you need every bit of it.'

For the first two or three weeks after his return from the course, the new sub-postmaster will be given a full-time Post Office counter worker to help and advise him. Then he is on his own in the store.

The sub-postmaster will be subject to checks from Post Office staff to make sure that he is doing his job properly and handling efficiently the quite considerable sums of money passing over his counter each week.

10 Joining the Post Office

There are a number of different ways of joining the staff of the Post Office. Many young men and a number of young women are taken on the collection and delivery staff each year as postmen and postwomen.

There are usually vacancies in this department. A number of trainees do not complete their basic training. The main reasons for this are that young people do not always like starting work as early as five in the morning. The long walks in all weathers also put a number of people off the job.

Those postmen who have been doing the job for some time, however, seem to enjoy the responsibility and comparative freedom of collecting and delivering the mail.

This is particularly true of the men who have come into the Post Office service from other jobs in factories, offices and the armed forces, and who have something with which to compare the postman's round.

'You're providing a service, and you're on your own a lot,' said one postman, speaking for many. 'And when the weather's nice you've got the bonus of being outside in the sun.'

A young man may join as a postal cadet and then proceed to postman and postman higher grade. There are opportunities for him to work his way up to supervisory posts, especially if he improves his educational qualifications by

A postal cadet will learn all about the different jobs in a post office.

A routine has to be maintained in the sorting office to prevent pile-ups of mail.

Issuing passports is just one of the many services performed by high street post offices.

sparetime study.

Counter staff need better educational backgrounds than those joining as postmen. G.C.E. passes at 'O' level are required. Successful candidates are sent on an intensive course during which they are taught about all the forms and procedures necessary to work behind the counter in a post office.

Both men and women work as counter staff. Most of them find the job tiring, and the pressure at certain times of the day when queues start winding round the building can be wearing.

Potential managers are recruited by the Post Office if they have university degrees or G.C.E. passes at 'A' level. Usually about 700 trainee managers are taken on every year.

A young manager may be sent to work in the Post Office's headquarters in London or out to one of the regional headquarters or head post offices. He will help to plan and carry out policy, or work in a specialist branch like Finance or Personnel.

11 Parcel Post

The Post Office is in competition with other carriers when it comes to transporting parcels. This means that it has to offer a number of different services.

In the post offices the parcel counter is not the most popular with staff members. 'It's so complicated,' said one assistant.

Weighing and stamping the parcels that are brought in needs a great deal of concentration. A parcel may not weigh more than 10 kg or be more than 1.07 m long.

If the parcel comes to pieces once it is in transit, it may never reach its destination. At the Mount Pleasant sorting office in London there is a division known as 'Heartbreak Corner'. This is where the parcels which have disintegrated end up.

The counter assistant also has to be prepared to answer all sorts of questions about the contents and the possible progress of the parcels being handed over the counter.

To help her she can refer to a specially prepared book, *Post Office Guide*. From this, for example, she can tell customers that it is forbidden to send binoculars to Abu Dhabi; that it should take about six weeks for a parcel to reach the Balearic Islands by ship; that £125 is the most for which an airmail parcel to St. Lucia may be insured.

The Post Office may also enter into a special arrangement with businesses to pick up and transport its packages. If more than twenty parcels are posted a day, there is no fee for the collection. Instead of having to weigh the parcels and buy stamps for each one, the firm receives a bill from the Post Office later.

The Post Office has divided the country up into a number of regions and zones. Parcels travelling within a zone cost less to post. One zone consists of Derbyshire and

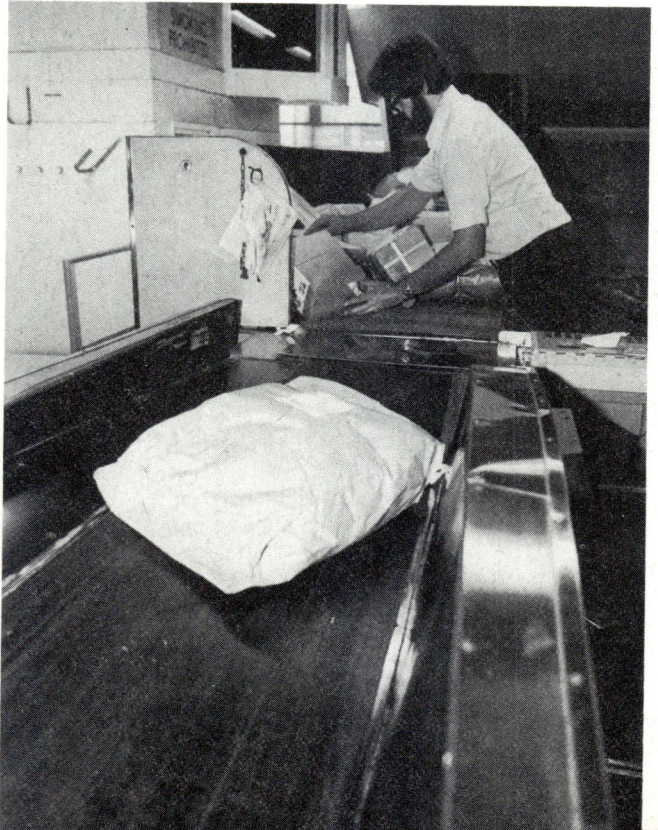

The Post Office has to compete with private carriers for the handling of parcels.

Nottinghamshire, another of Dorset and Hampshire, and so on.

There are also different methods of transporting goods within these zones. The Nightrider system, which applies throughout the Greater London area, will deliver overnight any parcels up to 20 kg in weight. The Contract Local Delivery service will deliver the next day anything collected within a particular zone. For cross-country distribution the Post Office vans will link up with a special air service.

These bulky parcels have been checked and are on their way out of the sorting office.

Postmen have to be prepared to lift heavy weights in the course of their work.

12 Save It!

The Post Office operates a number of different savings schemes on behalf of the government Perhaps the best known is the premium bond system. This is a unique method of saving. The holders of bonds earn no interest on their investment. Instead they stand a chance of winning a prize of as much as £250,000.

The bonds are sold over post office counters. They cost £1 each, but at least five must be bought at a time. The most bonds that one person can own is ten thousand.

Seven per cent of all the money invested in premium bonds each year is put aside to provide prizes for the draws. Each month there is a first prize of £250,000 and many smaller prizes. In addition, there is a weekly draw in which there is a first prize of £100,000, a second prize of £50,000 and a third prize of £25,000.

The premium bond service is run by the Post Office from Lytham St. Annes, Lancashire. The draws for the bonds winning prizes are made by

A postman receives the keys of the postboxes on his round from the registered-mail office.

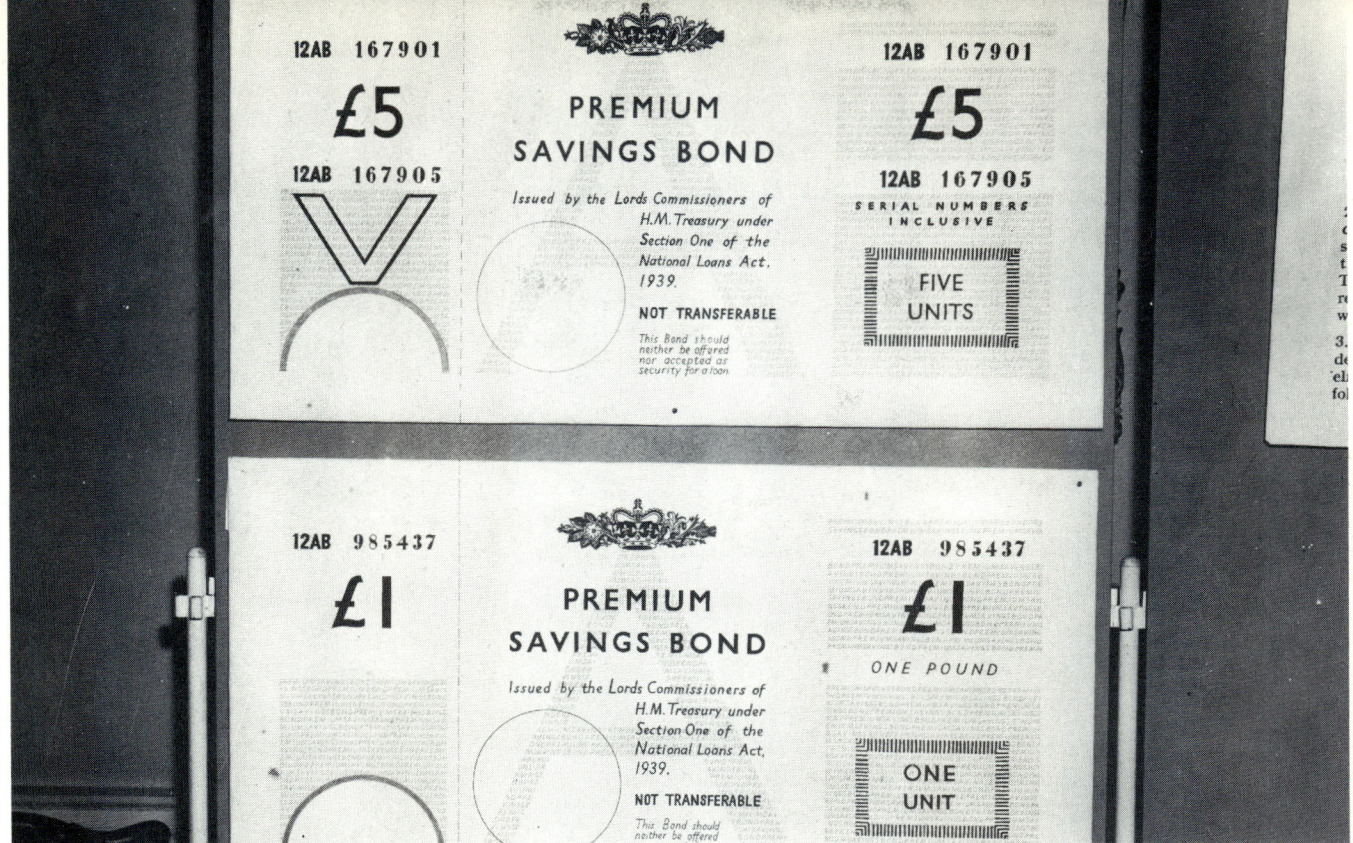

A premium bond holder can win up to £250,000 if 'Ernie' selects his number.

a piece of electronic technology known for short as 'Ernie'. This stands for Electronic Random Number Indicator Equipment.

Other schemes to help people save which are operated by the Post Office include the National Girobank and the National Savings Bank.

The Girobank is operated just like any other banking service. Customers are given chequebooks when they open an account. For the first six months they may cash cheques for up to £50 at either of two post offices they nominate. After that they may apply for a cheque card which enables them to cash cheques at post offices all over the country.

An advantage that the Giro has over other banking systems is that post offices are open longer than most banks, and cheques may be cashed at any time during shopping hours.

The National Savings Bank, also operated from high street post offices, is open to everyone over the age of seven. There are two types of N.S.B. account. The ordinary account pays interest of five per cent. Up to £100 may be withdrawn at any time. The investment account pays interest of 14.5 per cent, but one month's notice of withdrawal has to be given.

13 Finance

Great sums of money are handled by the different branches of the Post Office every year. In 1980–81, the organization had an income of £6,579.7 million. It made a profit of £208.7 million.

Over £180 million of this came from the telecommunications section. A little over £29 million profit was made by the postal services. The National Girobank made a loss of £1.8 million, but much of this was due to a special tax levied on the deposits of all banks by the government.

This was the last year that the various groups were to report together. In October 1981, they became two separate units, British Telecom and the Post Office (which includes the National Girobank).

The announcement of these figures aroused a certain amount of controversy. As a nationalized concern, the Post Office is watched very closely by the Department of Industry. The Department of Industry expressed disappointment that profits were down thirty per cent.

A 'watchdog' body, the Post Office Users National Council, complained that postal and telephone charges were going to go up even though a profit had been declared. It also disapproved of the way in which Post Office salaries were going up, pointing out that there

Executives can keep an eye on sorters through windows in the sorting room's wall.

were now 358 executives earning more than £20,000 a year.

For its part, the Post Office announced that even in a time of recession it had made a profit for five consecutive years, when most national postal services were suffering losses. It made the point that the Japanese postal organization, for example, had lost £545 million in a year, while the West German service had made a loss of £430 million.

The Post Office went on to explain the sheer size of its organization and the volume of work carried out. In 1981 there were over 27 million telephones in service, making 16,800 million local calls and 3,335 million trunk calls a year.

The critics of the service said that there had been a falling off in the services provided, that the Post Office had not reached its target of delivering ninety per cent of first-class mail on the day after it had been posted. It was also stated that in 1968, before the two-tier system had been introduced, it had cost 4d (1.7p) to post a letter, but that by 1981 a first-class stamp cost 14p.

A familiar sign! In 1980, the Post Office earned £236 million by carrying mail.

The Post Office spends vast amounts on such things as wages, new equipment and lighting.

14 The First Postal Services

Blazing arrows, drums, smoke signals and exhausted runners bearing messages in cleft sticks were just some of the forerunners of the Post Office we know today.

From the dawn of time men have tried to communicate with one another by passing on messages. Red Indian warriors sent burning arrows into the sky to signal the approach of enemies. African jungle drums beat out warnings in code.

In the time of Elizabeth I the English feared a Spanish invasion. Great bonfires, called beacons, were built on hilltops across the country. As soon as the Spanish Armada was sighted in the English Channel, torches were put to the brushwood to spread the warning.

But long before that the world's first regular postal service seems to have been set up. It was established in the great empire of the Persian monarch Xerxes, over 2,500 years ago.

The lands of Xerxes extended from the Mediterranean to the borders of Asia and Europe. In an effort to keep in touch with his governors throughout his sprawling empire, the ruler began a primitive postal service.

His messengers were sent out on foot, mule and camel to take the royal commands to the outer provinces. This became a regular system and was continued by the Persians for hundreds of years. It was said of these messengers that the king's mail was carried more swiftly than the birds of the air could travel.

Other rulers of the ancient world copied this method of keeping great kingdoms together. Before long it was discovered that it was more efficient to have regular stopping places along the routes where fresh messengers or beasts of burden could take over.

From these royal systems it was only a short

The predecessors of these postmen carried mail in chariots, on horseback and in wagons.

Hilltop bonfires announced the arrival of the Spanish Armada in Elizabeth I's reign.

step to the growth of postal services for the use of ordinary people.

The Egyptians set up such a network of messengers. They had been among the pioneers of writing, having perfected a form of picture-script painted with brushes on to strips of papyrus made from reeds.

The Egyptian messengers had a dangerous task. Of one it was written: 'Before departing, he maketh over his fortune to his children from fear of the Asiatics and the wild animals.'

An Express Letter sent to Colonel Fairfax by his cousin in May 1639.

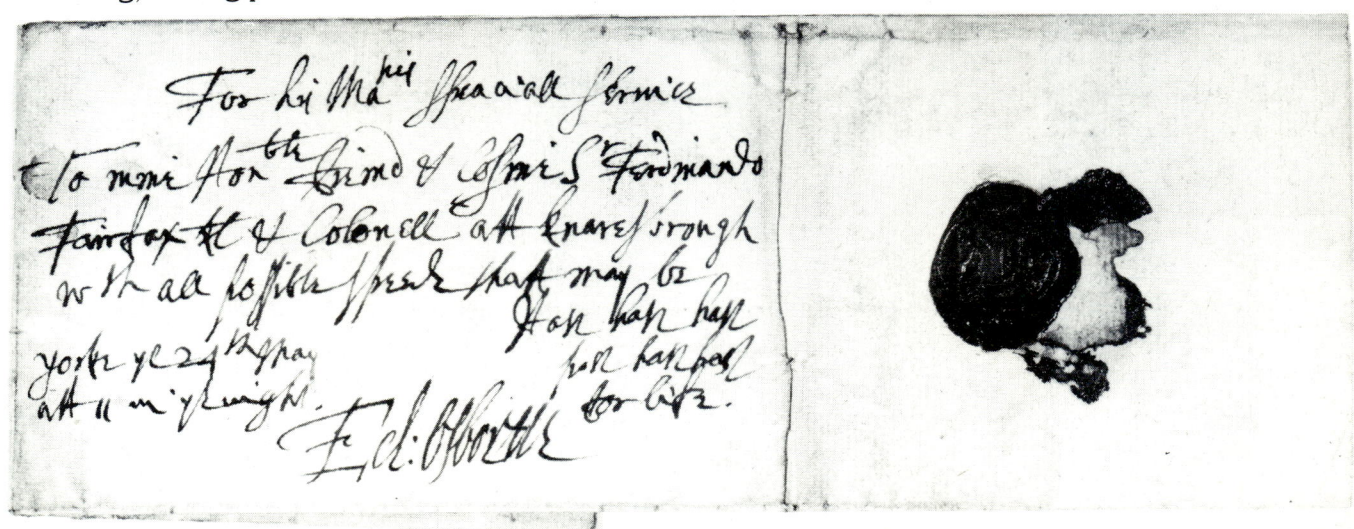

15 The Postal Services Develop

The citizens of the small states of ancient Greece prided themselves on their physical fitness. Their messengers scorned the use of horses and travelled swiftly on foot from city to city.

Perhaps the best known of these athletic couriers was Pheidippides. When a Persian army invaded Greece in 490 B.C., he is said to have run for a day and a night from Athens to Sparta to fetch help.

It was the Romans, however, who made the next great advance in the history of the postal service. The Roman Empire extended as far as Britain in one direction and the borders of India in the other.

Fine roads were built across this empire. A postal service was introduced under the care of paid officials. The messengers drove light chariots over the roads at great speed. To distinguish them, so that other road-users would get out of the way, the Roman messengers wore hats with feathers stuck in them. This is where we

Messengers in speedy chariots kept all corners of the Roman Empire in touch.

A contemporary illustration of postman in the early part of the seventeenth century.

get our modern phrase 'a feather in his cap', to mean that someone has done well.

The Romans also gave the service its name. The word *post* comes from the Latin *positus*, meaning fixed. It referred to the official stations along the postal routes, where fresh horses were kept for the messengers.

By the sixth century A.D., the Roman Empire was coming to an end, conquered by the barbarians. The great Roman roads fell into disrepair and the postal services were abandoned.

For hundreds of years the sending and receiving of messages became a haphazard affair. In the Middle Ages in England, such services were organized mainly by the king, the Church and wealthy merchants.

Various monarchs took an interest in the postal service. King John dressed his messengers in a special livery. King Henry VIII created the office of Master of the King's Post. It was this official's task to organize the mounted postboys and the post houses along their routes.

Because these postboys sometimes dawdled along the poor roads, a system of post-marks was devised. Letters were dated so that people could see how long it took for messages to be delivered.

Ordinary people had to send their letters as best they could. They paid coach drivers and the owners of delivery wagons to help.

Henry VIII, who reigned from 1491 to 1547, created the office of Master of the King's Post.

16 A Postal Service for All

In 1635, Charles I made Thomas Witherings his Chief Postmaster. This efficient administrator re-organized the English postal system.

Witherings set up six main post roads across Britain. Smaller post roads ran off the main ones. It cost two pence to send a letter up to 120 kilometres. The person receiving the message had to pay for it.

More than a hundred years later a London merchant called William Dockwra set up a private postal service in the capital. His messengers collected letters and took them to one of five sorting offices. From the sorting offices the letters went on to their destinations in London for a fee of one penny a message.

Dockwra's system was so successful that the government of the day took it away from him and made it an official postal service.

In 1784, John Palmer produced a specially designed mailcoach which could travel up to twelve kilometres an hour. Inns were used as

The Bath and Bristol mailcoach in 1784. A Post Office guard accompanied the driver.

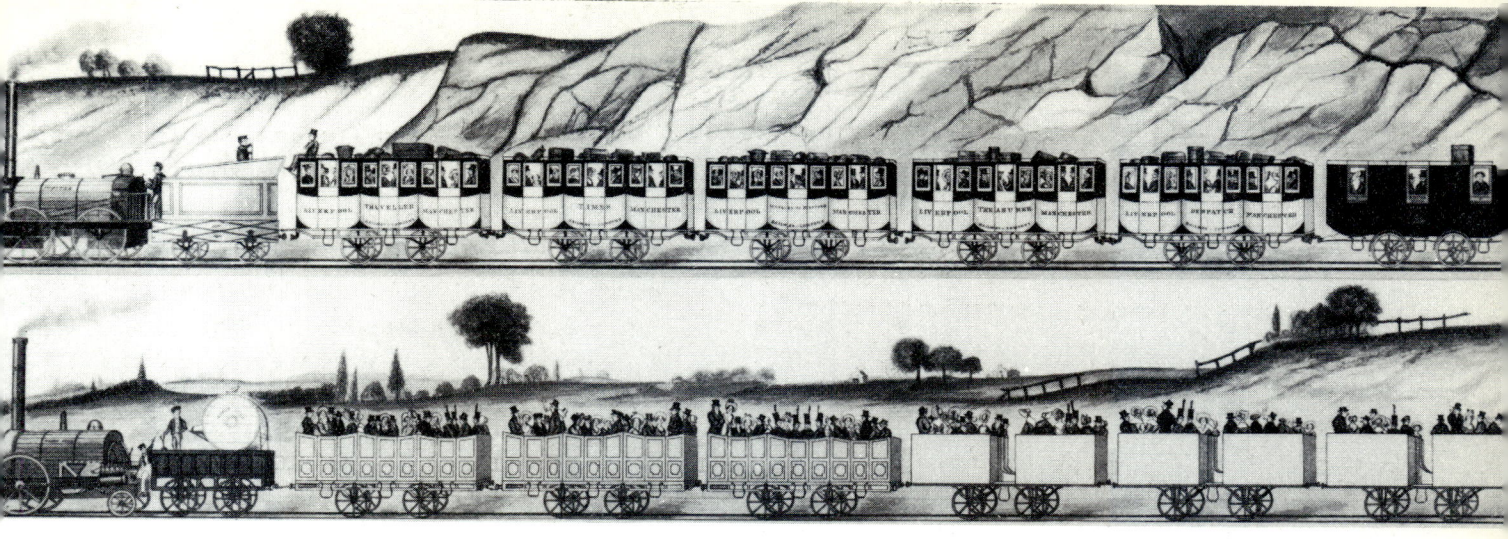

The Liverpool and Manchester railway was carrying mail by the end of 1831.

staging posts. Before long there were as many as twenty-seven postal routes out of London, spreading all over the country.

A guard employed by the Post Office travelled on each mailcoach. This man wore a uniform of a scarlet coat with blue lapels, a blue waistcoat and a hat with a gold band. He carried a blunderbuss and had a horn and a set of pistols close at hand. Such guards were necessary as the roads in the eighteenth century were plagued by armed robbers, known as highwaymen.

The heyday of the mailcoaches lasted little more than fifty years. Then they were replaced by the fast and reliable railway trains. The first mailtrain ran in 1830 and only eight years later the last mailcoach set out on its final journey.

Ten years after the first mailtrain, in 1840, Rowland Hill introduced his famous penny post. This was a system by which people wishing to send a letter could do so by buying a penny stamp to stick on the message.

Such a cheap method of sending mail was so popular that within a few years more than half a million letters were being sent and delivered in every twelve-month period. In 1860, Rowland Hill, the pioneer of the modern postal service, was knighted.

Sir Rowland Hill originated the system of paying for mail with stamps.

17 In the Mail

Mail-carrying services have crossed Britain for hundreds of years. Just as they do today, these services have carried all sorts of messages.

Much of what we know about the history of our country has been learned from these old letters, faithfully delivered and then kept.

A picture of life in monasteries has been built up from the parchments passed among the monks in the tenth and eleventh centuries. Each monastery would add its own news to the scroll before sending it on its way. Some of these messages were over nine metres long.

A few hundred years later, a Norfolk family, called the Pastons, exchanged many letters which have been preserved. From these historians have established how people worked and played in the Middle Ages.

Some letters have been sent great distances in order to right a wrong, or to express a point of view. In the nineteenth century Robert Louis Stevenson, author of *Treasure Island*, was living on the Pacific island of Samoa. Civil war broke out on the island. One of the claimants to the throne was then banished by the German authorities.

In an effort to see that justice was done, Stevenson sent a series of letters, protesting against the decision, all the way to *The Times* newspaper in London. The letters reached England, were published and caused an uproar; leading to questions being asked in the House of Commons.

Some unusual articles have also gone through the post. In 1909, the Prime Minister of Britain refused to see some suffragettes who wanted to discuss the question of votes for women.

Two women then 'posted' themselves to 10 Downing Street, as the Post Office undertook to deliver livestock as well as packages. They were refused admittance and returned as 'dead letters'!

A monk in the twelfth century. Monastries passed on news to each other on scrolls.

Love letters, threatening letters – all sorts of mail passes through a sorting office.

Today the Post Office appreciates the importance to both the senders and the recipients of the millions of letters posted each year. Business agreements, packages containing valuables, even proposals of marriage go through the post.

According to the *Guinness Book of Records*, the longest letter ever sent in this country was written by a young lady in Southsea to her boyfriend. It was more than 1,200 metres long!

There are some 40,000 pillar boxes in Britain. This is the newest type, introduced in 1980.

18 The Post Office and Railways

The Post Office has always been quick to use all new forms of transport. Almost from the beginning of Britain's railway system, the Post Office authorities recognized the potential of fast-moving, reliable trains running to timetables and crossing the country in all directions.

Today the bulk of Britain's mail is moved by train. At the larger stations there are postmen who work full-time loading and unloading the mailbags from trains and seeing them on their way to sorting offices.

Life on these crowded, bustling platforms is hectic. Time passes quickly for the postal workers; but some of them find their surroundings confining, with never a minute to leave the station before another train pulls in. 'I sometimes think I'm going to live and die on this platform,' said one railway postman grimly.

A number of postal workers may be found on trains as they speed through the night. Such trains are known as Travelling Post Offices (T.P.O.s). The first of these was introduced in 1838. It was a horsebox transformed into a mobile sorting office and joined on to a train running between Manchester and Birmingham.

This was a great success. Before long the Post Office had introduced a number of these

Some 75% of letter-mail and 92% of parcel-mail is carried by rail at some stage of its journey.

A sorter in a Travelling Post Office sorts mail as the train travels through the night.

T.P.O.s. Today there are some fifty mobile sorting offices. The mail is loaded on board and, as the train travels though the night, the sorters put the letters into the correct pigeonholes ready for their destination.

For a long time, until 1971, all along the route of some T.P.O.s, mailbags were taken on board by being attached to metal frames along the side of the track. These bags were dropped into nets lowered from the passing train. At the same time, sacks of sorted mail were transferred from the moving train to the outstretched arms of the metal frames, to await collection.

The sorters on a T.P.O. start work as soon as they board the train. They open the mailbags and begin to put the letters into the correct racks on the board in front of them. Until the mailbags are needed, they are kept in wire cages on board the train. The empty sacks are hung on hooks opposite the letter racks.

It was in 1966 that the most famous T.P.O. of all left a platform at Glasgow railway station on its way south to London.

19 The Great Train Robbery

Early on an August morning in 1966 a small group of desperate and determined men waited in a quiet part of Buckinghamshire to rob a mail-train.

At about three o'clock in the morning the train could be heard approaching. It was the overnight express from Glasgow to Euston station in London.

In addition to its contingent of passengers, the diesel engine was pulling a number of mobile sorting offices, with about seventy sorters at work as the train thundered through the night.

It was the second coach that interested the waiting robbers. It was known as a High Value Package Coach. Inside one of its padlocked wire cages was a pile of bags. Each bag was full of banknotes, sent down from Scottish banks to London.

One of the criminals had tampered with the signal, knowing that this would make the train stop. The plan worked. The train pulled to a halt and the fireman climbed down and walked along the track to see what was wrong. He was siezed by members of the gang.

Others in the party stormed the engine, coshing the driver. When the dazed man had recovered, he was forced to drive the engine a little farther down the track to a bridge. Most of the coaches had been uncoupled, leaving only some of them still attached to the engine. One of the coaches still coupled was the one containing the sacks of banknotes.

When the engine pulled up by the bridge and the waiting lorry, the robbers broke down the door of the coach. There were five sorters inside. They tried unsuccessfully to keep out the

criminals by piling sacks against the door.

The robbers jumped over the sacks and ordered the sorters to lie on the floor. They then broke into the cage and started hauling out the sacks stored inside.

Forming a human chain the train robbers passed 120 sacks down the embankment to the lorry. They then drove off to a deserted farmhouse. Here they discovered that they had stolen £2.5 million.

Eventually most of the robbers were arrested and sentenced to long prison sentences, although much of the money was never recovered. The theft went down in history as the Great Train Robbery.

The Glasgow to Euston express was held up in 1966 and £2.5 million robbed from it.

20 The Post Office Railway

Some twenty-five metres below the streets of London, the Post Office has built its own underground railway.

The service was first planned for 1913. Even then the streets of London were so crowded that it was becoming more and more difficult to transport mail across the capital from the sorting offices to the railway stations and back again.

The idea of a network of railway lines beneath the city was accepted and plans drawn up. The outbreak of the First World War meant that the

The Post Office railway carries more than six million letters each day under London's streets.

opening had to be put off. It was 1927 before the Post Office railway came into service. It has been running ever since.

The route runs from Paddington station to Whitechapel. It is open from 10 a.m. on Monday morning until 8 a.m. on Sunday. There is a two-hour break every day while the track is inspected and maintained.

Along the route there are seven stations. Each has a platform rather like that of an underground station. The two main-line stations feeding the system are Paddington and Liverpool Street. The other stations are intermediary stops along the way.

The longest platform is Mount Pleasant, about 100 metres in length. The shortest platform is only 30 metres long.

Bags of mail descend to the platform from the sorting offices above by lift or by chute and are loaded on to the trains. Other bags are unloaded and sent up to the sorting offices.

Some 38,000 bags of mail a year are transported on the underground trains. The trains do not have drivers or any other Post Office workers on board. They are controlled electrically by operators in switch-cabins on some of the platforms.

These operators supervise switchboards which take the trains at a speed of about forty kilometres an hour along the tracks. The tracks slope upwards as they approach the platforms, slowing the trains down before they are brought to a halt.

The trains appear at the platforms at four-minute intervals. Each one draws one or more cars. There are four mailbag containers on each car. A container may carry fifteen bags of letter-mail or six bags of parcel-mail.

The Post Office railway transports 35,000 mailbags each day in its containers.

21 Other Transport

In order to deliver the mail as quickly and safely as possible, the Post Office uses many different forms of transport.

As early as 1897 it was experimenting with steam-driven vehicles. Soon after the end of the First World War a fleet of motor delivery vans was introduced. Today, with a total approaching 30,000 vehicles, the Post Office operates the largest transport organization in the country.

In some rural areas of Britain, the Post Office delivers its letters and parcels in minibuses. These buses also provide another service by taking fare-paying customers to remote areas on the postal routes.

The first airmail service operated between Hendon and Windsor in 1911, to mark the coronation of King George V. Within eight years there was a regular air route from England to France. Today millions of letters every year are transported by jumbo jet and Concorde to and from London's Heathrow Airport.

Many postal workers are involved in loading and unloading the mail at this airport. They have to work closely with the police stationed at Heathrow because of the high rate of pilfering there. Bags of airmail are much sought-after by thieves.

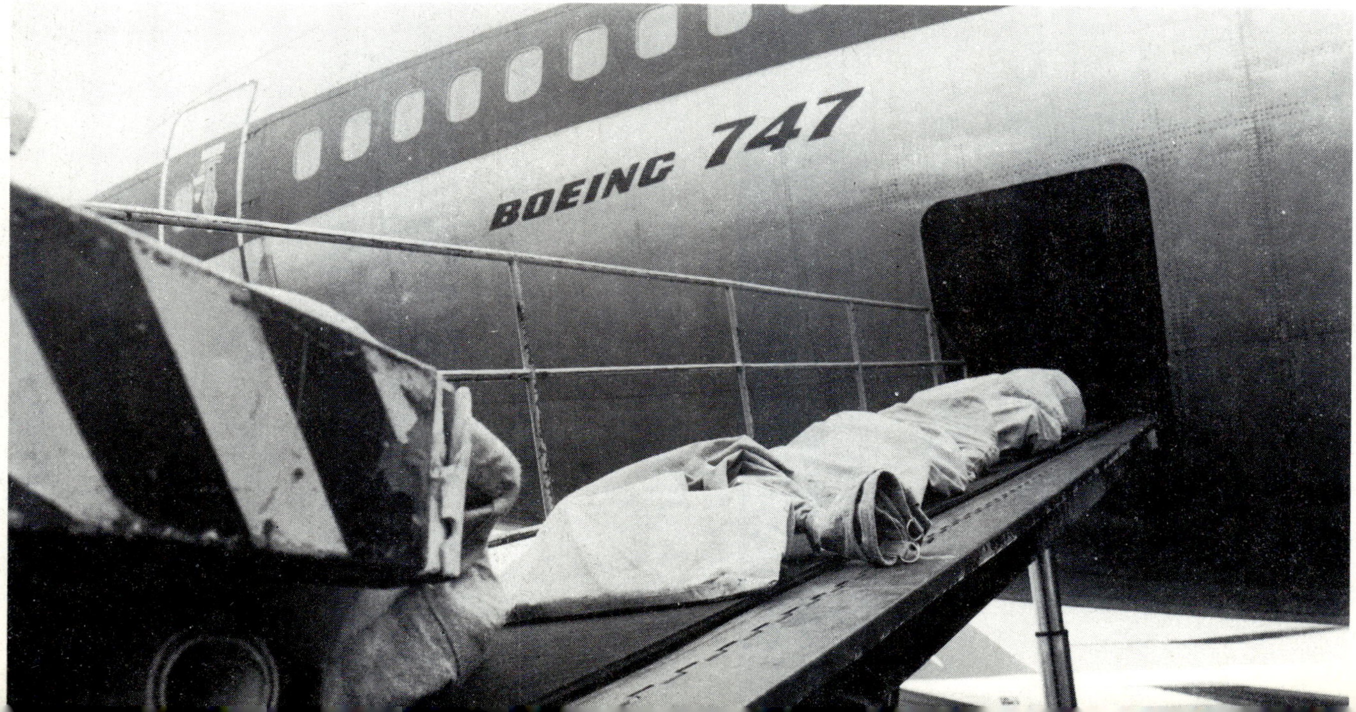

Airmail being loaded into the hold of a British Airways Boeing 747 at Heathrow Airport.

Sailors loading sacks of mail on to a steamship at Brindisi, Italy in 1872.

This Postbus delivers mail in rural areas. It can carry up to nine fare-paying passengers.

Another hazard of working for the Post Office at this airport is the chance of explosives being smuggled on or off airliners. If any airport worker has any suspicions about a packet, it is placed with great care into a van and taken to a decompression chamber on the far side of the airport, where it may be investigated.

Fourteen different airports are used to fly airmail on long-distance routes inside Britain. The Flying Royal Mail Service was started in 1979 to make sure that letters bearing a first-class stamp would be delivered a day after they were posted.

The Post Office hires six different airlines to deliver this airmail. Each airline collects and delivers letters from the airports. In 1981, a Dan-Air Hawker Siddeley with a crew of three and carrying three tonnes of airmail crashed in a cornfield in Leicestershire, killing all on board.

Ships, too, take their share of mail to and from Britain. Much of this seamail passes through the Overseas Mail Office, near London's docks.

22 Designing Postage Stamps

Many modern postage stamps are beautiful works of art considerably reduced in size. As much care is given to their design and production as to the execution of the landscapes and portraits hanging on art gallery walls.

The world's first printed postage stamps were made in Britain. The first illustration was the head of Queen Victoria on the famous Penny Black.

Modern postage stamps are much more colourful and have a far greater variety of designs than those of a century ago.

The subjects to be illustrated on British stamps are the responsibility of a branch of the Post Office known as the Postal Marketing Department.

In the course of a year more than two hundred people and organizations put forward their suggestions for illustrations for new issues of stamps.

All these ideas and others brought up within the Post Office itself are examined by the department. The best are placed before the

Artist Peter Oxenham working in his studio on the designs for the horses stamps.

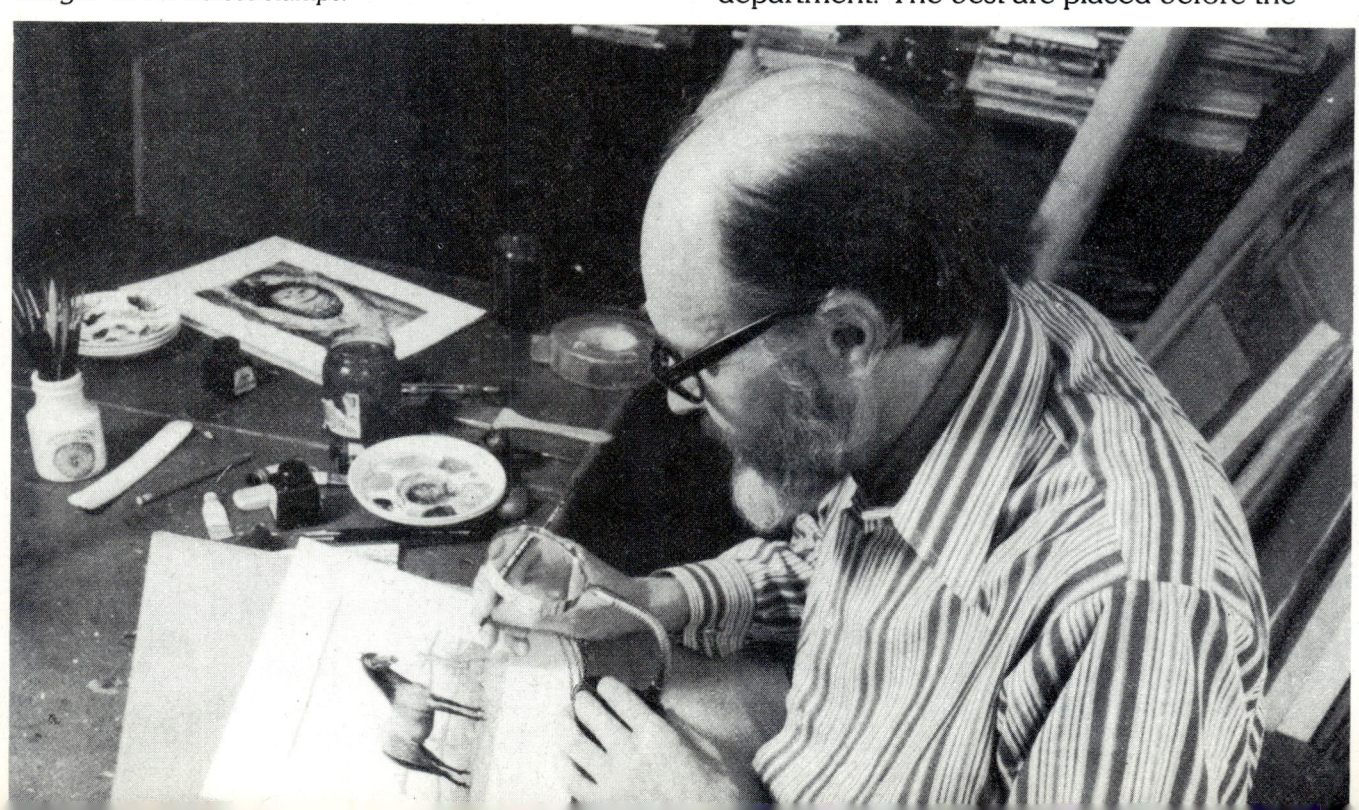

Many modern postage stamps are works of art considerably reduced in size.

Stamp Advisory Committee, a group of men and women from inside and outside the Post Office.

Eventually, after considerable discussions, the subjects for the forthcoming issues are agreed upon. They may represent anniversaries, famous events, notable people, or any number of other subjects.

Among the hundreds of topics selected for stamp issues have been the centenary of the birth of Sir Winston Churchill, the Year of the Child, and British trees.

The Post Office's Director of Design then approaches a number of artists and invites them to submit designs for the proposed subject of the next issue.

A number of artists specialize in stamp design; others may be approached because the Design Director approves of their work or knows that they are interested in the particular topic chosen.

Each artist is given about six weeks in which to produce a design four times the size of the actual proposed stamp. All the designs are then set before the Stamp Advisory Committee and one of them is accepted.

The successful artist then does a great deal of research into the subject before he produces the illustrations for all the stamps in the new issue.

The final designs for the stamp have to be approved by the minister in charge of the Post Office and then go before the Queen before they are accepted for production.

23 Producing the Stamps

When the Penny Black was first designed in 1840, the head of Queen Victoria, reproduced from a portrait, was etched by engravers laboriously transferring the likeness on to steel plates. The work was said to be so detailed and intricate that it took the best part of a week to complete the monarch's eyes alone.

Today the printing process is such an intricate and technical one that the printer is called in at an early stage to give advice. He is regarded as a partner in the task of completing the production of a new issue of stamps.

As a rule the printer is first asked to contribute his skills when the Stamp Advisory Committee has selected the design to be turned into a stamp. The original painting has been photographed and reduced to the size of a postage stamp, to give an idea of how it will look.

Usually the printer will use four or five colours in the production of a stamp, after consultation with the artist and the Post Office designers. More than five colours may be used, but this is a very complicated process.

When all the designs have been approved the printer can go ahead with producing them. He uses a process called photogravure. This involves the use of a number of cylinders, each printing in a different colour on to gummed paper.

At some stage in the printing process the perforations, along which the stamps can be detached from a sheet, are added. The stamps are then produced by the printing machines. Assistants inspect each sheet emerging from the machines to make sure that there are no misprints. Any faulty issues are destroyed.

The approved sheets of stamps are then distributed to post offices up and down the country. Some are sent to head office to be transferred on to first-day covers. These are

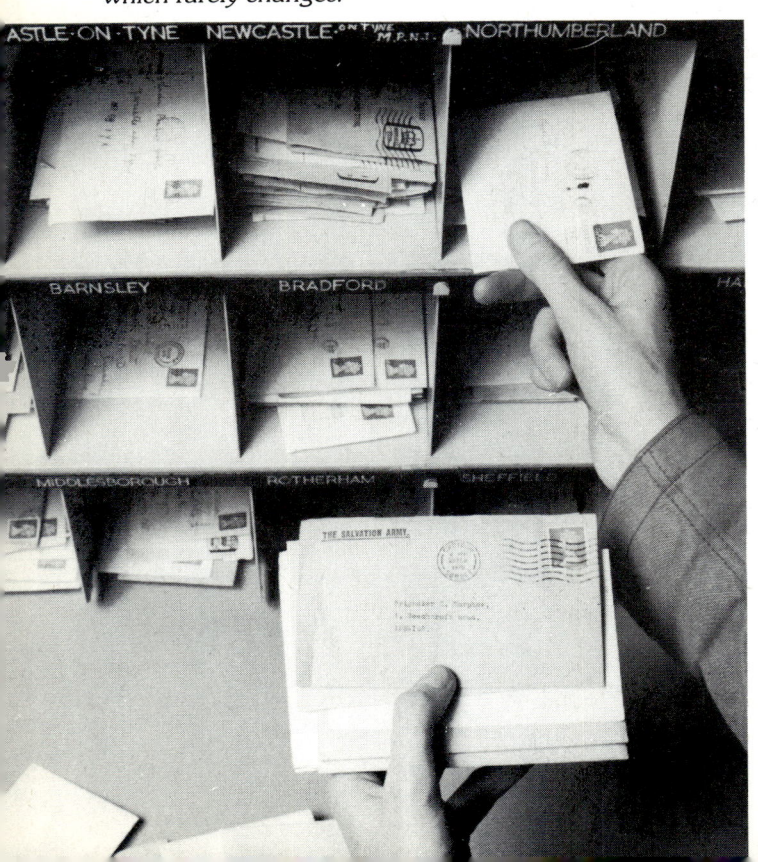

Most of our mail carries 'definitive' stamps, the design of which rarely changes.

placed on a specially prepared envelope and stamped with the date of their issue. First-day covers are intended for collectors.

In addition to the nine or ten special issues produced every year, the Post Office continues to prepare and produce its 'definitive' standard stamps, bearing the head of the Queen. These hardly change from year to year.

The Penny Black, the world's first adhesive postage stamp, was placed on sale in May 1840. In all 66 million Penny Blacks were printed before they were replaced by Penny Reds in January 1841.

24 Stamp Collecting

The Post Office has a section to help people who collect British postage stamps. Based at High Wycombe, it is called the Stamp Bug Club.

Six times a year it issues to members a glossy newspaper which, among other news items and articles, describes the latest issues of British stamps.

In addition, a number of post offices have philatelic sales counters where new issues may be purchased by collectors.

The world's first postage stamp, the famous

Some post offices have sections where collectors can buy new issues of stamps.

Penny Black, was produced in 1840, when Rowland Hill introduced his penny postage system. More than sixty million of them were sold. Today a Penny Black in good condition may fetch £100.

The first stamp collector of whom there is any record was a young woman who advertized in *The Times* newspaper in 1841, only a year after the first stamps were issued. This young woman asked people to send her any used Penny Black stamps that they might have, so that she could paper a dressing-room wall with them. It is said that she received 16,000 stamps as a result of her appeal.

Within a few years, by which time other nations were also producing postage stamps, collecting had become a hobby. The first real catalogue of stamps was published in Paris in 1861. It listed almost 1,500 stamps.

Today there are so many millions of stamps available that collectors have to specialize, or concentrate on one particular kind of stamp. Some collectors do this by country, gathering together examples of stamps produced by one nation, but even this is a staggering task.

It is more common for collectors to select stamps by themes. This means that they choose stamps based on one particular subject – sport, perhaps, or wildlife.

All collectors hope to discover a really valuable stamp in the way that a boy in British Guiana did in 1873. The stamp he came across, the only remaining British Guiana one-cent issue of 1856, was valued only a few years ago at three hundred thousand pounds.

Prior to the existence of stamps for letters, people paid postmen to deliver their mail.

Stamp collecting, however, does not have to be an expensive hobby. All that is needed is an album in which to keep the stamps, hinges with which to amount them in the book, tweezers for handling the stamps and a magnifying glass with which to examine them.

25 British Telecom

For much of this century the Post Office was responsible for the telephone service and later the telex system. Now, however, British Telecom has taken over a great deal of what used to be the technological side of Britain's communications system.

Many telephone exchanges are still attached to post offices, but they are administered by British Telecom. The service maintains twenty-five million telephones making more than fifty million calls a day.

It has more than 234,000 workers, including operators, technicians, engineers, salesmen and executives. There are sixty-one different telephone areas, each under the control of a general manager.

Some exchanges are still manned by operators. Many are automatic, with complex groupings of machinery and technology. When someone makes a telephone call by dialling a number, the action sends a series of electrical impulses along the telephone wires to the exchange.

These impulses work a switch which then directs the call along the wires to the house or office for which the call was intended.

A telephone call made outside the district served by the local exchange is called a trunk call. Such a call is relayed to the telephone exchange in the required district.

Places a long way away may be dialled directly by Subscriber Trunk Dialling (S.T.D.). A group of numbers stands for the exchange in the area wanted. This group of numbers is dialled before the number of the subscriber wanted.

Telephones are also used to pass on telegrams whenever possible. Another service is the telex one. Each telex customer has a special machine in his office. A number is dialled, rather like operating a telephone. Then a message is typed

A telephone operator at her switchboard at the turn of the century.

on one machine. The same message appears on the receiver's telex machine. This system is known as teleprinting.

School leavers with G.C.E. or good C.S.E. passes in suitable subjects may enter British Telecom as trainee technicians.

They serve an apprenticeship, with time off to attend college. They are given the opportunity to become technician officers, installing and maintaining telephone equipment in the automatic exchanges. Technician officers who gain added qualifications may progress to the position of engineer or executive engineer.

A modern-day operator at a cordless telephone exchange. It is a push-button job now.

Electronic exchanges, such as this one below, are replacing electro-mechanical exchanges.

26 The Post Office Tower

Some high street post offices are small, others are big. Even the largest cannot approach the size of one building in London.

In 1966, the Post Office Tower was opened in London. This was before the Post Office and British Telecom became separate units.

The tower was designed to aid the transmission of telephone calls and television programmes. The tallest building in the capital, it was one of London's landmarks.

The tower was built of steel, concrete and glass. It was also designed with a central core of reinforced concrete. This was intended to keep the building steady in even the strongest wind. The structure tapered at the top and was exposed to the full force of the elements.

Every modern device has been included to shield the delicate technology inside the building. There are air-conditioning and refrigeration plants.

The lifts installed in the Post Office Tower are powerful enough to travel from the bottom to the top of the 189-metre tall building in just over half a minute.

The height was needed so that microwaves could be transmitted from the top of the tower. Microwaves are invisible beams which may carry both telephone calls and television programmes.

The microwaves travel in a straight line. If they are sent out from a great height no other building can interrupt them and they may travel as far as fifty kilometres. Then they must be picked up and sent on by other towers.

A telephone exchange inside the Post Office Tower is called the Mercury exchange. It receives telephone messages from all over the country and automatically sends them on to the people in London for whom they are intended.

The building also receives television

The Post Office Tower in London contains much modern technology.

programmes from both the B.B.C. and the I.T.V. companies. It beams them on to the transmitters from which they are sent out all over the country.

The great height of the tower was put to good use when a radar installation was placed at the top. This equipment gives warning of any approaching storms. At the same time it gathers other weather information.

Hundreds of men and women work in the building. These include administrators, engineers, technicians and maintenance staff.

Microwaves are transmitted all over Britain with the help of towers and aerials like these.

This tower, high above Birmingham's streets, helps to relay telephone calls and TV pictures.

27 The Future

It is difficult to forecast what may happen to the Post Office in the future. For hundreds of years it has had the right to be the only organization allowed to deliver letters in Britain. This sole right is called a monopoly.

Now it is possible that this monopoly may be challenged. If the government decides to allow other business firms to carry letter-mail this will mean more competition for the Post Office.

The Post Office is worried that, if private concerns are allowed to enter the letter-carrying business, they will only be interested in the profitable city collections and deliveries. The Post Office has pointed out that many of its rural deliveries lose money and are undertaken only as part of a nationwide service.

In the same way, the future of British Telecom has been debated. There have been reports that a part of the telephone and telex organization may not remain in government hands, but could be sold to a private concern.

No matter what happens to the administration of various branches of the Post Office, the service faces a number of very different problems.

It wants to take advantage of the technological advances being made to mechanize the mail and telephone system even further. It is looking for fresh ways of sorting the mail efficiently. At the moment, the Post Office points out, a letter, say, from Grimsby to Croydon may have to be sorted three times – in Grimsby, London and Croydon.

British Telecom, too, wants to take the telephone service even further forward. In the U.S.A. massive computers are being used to trace faults on the line, as well as to help callers get the right number. British Telecom plans to introduce such systems into this country.

At the same time, the Post Office is handicapped by lack of funds. There are not enough postmen to deliver letters and sort them. Rural telephone boxes are being run at a loss each year of £56 million. If they are withdrawn, however, they will isolate some lonely areas

This giant aerial in Cornwall transmits phone calls and TV pictures all over the world.

These 'billboard' aerials in Aberdeenshire link a North Sea oil rig with the mainland.

even more.

In spite of this lack of money, the Post Office is continuing to plan and carry out research. It is conscious that it is entering what will be a highly technological age. The Post Office hopes to keep pace with the events of such a world.

Phone calls and TV pictures are 'bounced off' satellites to another part of the world.

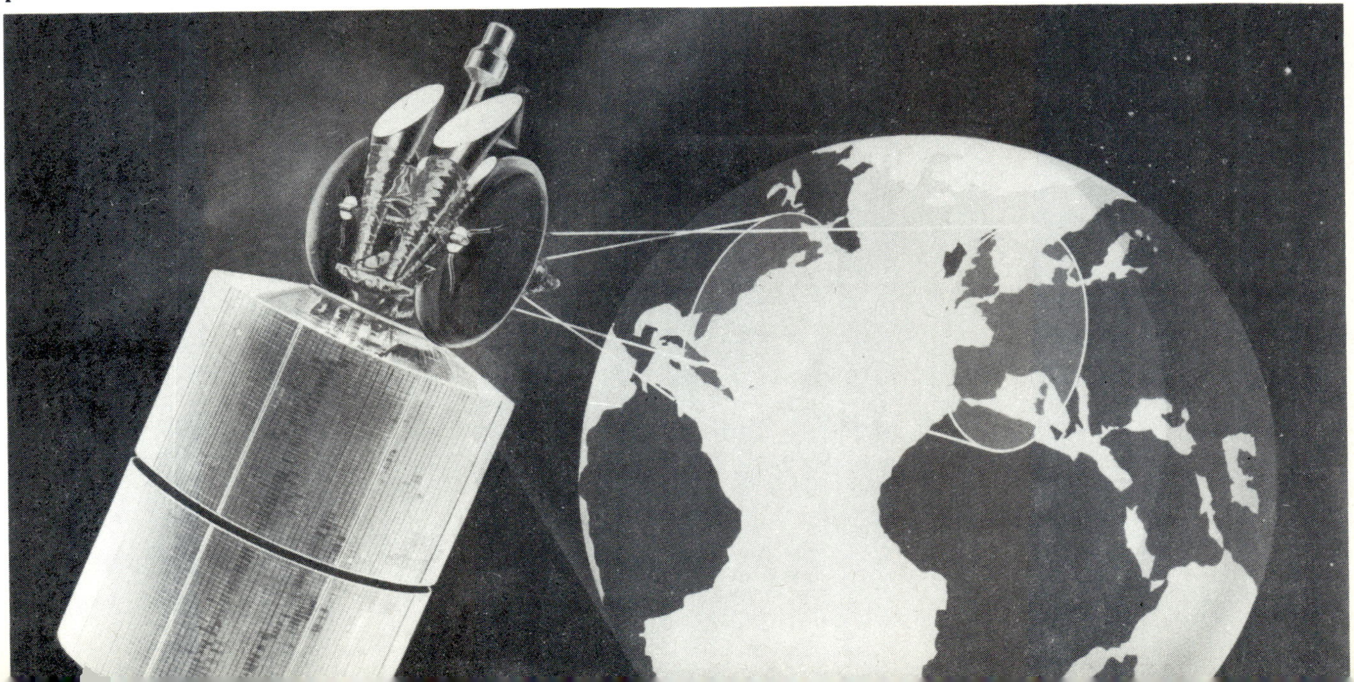

Facts and Figures

Income

	£m
Main services	
Mail	1,336.2
Agency	236.0
Other services	
Other PO businesses	131.1
Miscellaneous	4.7
	1,708.0

Staff numbers

Postal headquarters	3,470
Regional headquarters	3,468
National TV licence records office	561
Post offices	36,352
Sub-postmasters	21,056
Mail operations	125,225
Engineering	4,057
Motor transport	3,323
	197,542

Expenditure

	£m
Operating costs	1,310.3
Maintenance	35.7
Accommodation	59.4
Administration	65.9
Motor transport	53.7
Use of other PO businesses	42.7
Miscellaneous	115.2
	1,682.9

Salary expenditure

	£m
Salaries	1,094.3
Pensions	97.5
National Insurance	104.0
	1,295.8

Counter transactions

	Number (m)	Value (£m)
Sale of stamps	—	434.8
Postal orders issued	154.9	511.0
Telephone accounts paid	19.4	772.0
National Savings Bank: deposits	31.4	1,026.3
National Savings Bank: withdrawals	21.0	591.7
Premium bonds sold	3.8	95.5
Pensions paid	598.7	11,268.5
Child benefits paid	381.8	2,957.3
B & W TV licences issued	5.3	54.9
Colour TV licences issued	11.1	316.6
Passports issued	1.0	5.8

Mail posted

	Number (m)
Total correspondence posted	10,207.5
Total parcels handled	180.2
	10,387.7

Parcels posted

	Number (m)
Inland	171.1
Overseas	9.1
	180.2

Correspondence posted

	Number (m)
Inland	9,609.2
Overseas	598.3
	10,207.5

Motor transport

Number of vehicles in use	27,025
Total mileage	304,147,000

Payments for the transport of mail

	1980 £m
To contractors:	
Road	3.4
Rail	50.1
Sea	8.0
Air	42.5
	104.0

Further information

The Post Office provides a variety of educational project packs designed for use by teachers in the classroom. Teachers who would like copies of these packs should write to: Schools Officer, Room 127, 22–25 Finsbury Square, London EC2A 1PH (stating the age group of the children for whom the material is intended).

Important Dates and Events

1481   King Edward IV set up relay stations at intervals along the road from England to Scotland, where messengers could change their horses.

1517   King Henry VIII made Brian Tuke, later Sir Brian, the first Master of the Posts.

1635   Thomas Witherings introduced the first comprehensive postal service for the general public.

1680   William Dockwra organized a private, penny postal service for London and Westminster, employing more than fifty letter-carriers.

1685   Dockwra's service taken over by the government and incorporated into the state system.

1784   The first mailcoaches introduced; the first regular run being between Bristol and London. Some coaches reached a speed of twelve kilometres an hour.

1836   In terrible weather the Exeter mailcoach was dug out of snowdrifts five times.

1837   Rowland Hill urged postal reforms in his pamphlet *Post Office Reform: Its Importance and Practicability*.

1838   The last mailcoach made its run. The service was superseded by trains.

1840   Rowland Hill introduced his penny post. The Penny Black stamp was issued.

1853   The first letter collection boxes appeared in cities.

1860   Rowland Hill knighted by Queen Victoria for his contribution to the postal services.

1861   Postman's uniform designed: blue frock-coat and trousers with red pipings and facings, and a peaked cap.

1870   After two Acts of Parliament, the Post Office took over responsibility for the telegraphic service.

1874   The colour red adopted for pillar boxes.

1883   The parcel-post service was introduced.

1911   The first small airmail service began in Britain, to mark the coronation of King George V.

1912   The Post Office took over most private telephone systems.

1919   A fleet of motorized vans began to carry Post Office mail.

1927   The Post Office underground railway in London was opened.

1965   *Early Bird* satellite was launched to provide a regular telephone service between America and western Europe.

1966   The Post Office Tower was opened in London.

1969   The Post Office became a public corporation supervised by a Chairman and Board. The telecommunications part of the Post Office assumed responsibility for telephone and telex services.

1979   Flying Royal Mail Service inaugurated.

1981   The new Post Office corporation was created, with British Telecom a separate business responsible for telephone and telex services.

Glossary

Agency A business carried out by someone working for another person or organization.
Communications The act of passing on news and information. Telecommunications is passing on information by telephone, radio or television.
Computer A large machine which works out calculations automatically.
Deposit To place some money in a bank, post office, etc.
Executive A person responsible for the running of a business.
Licence A document giving official permission to do or to use something.
Nationalized industry An industry under the control of the government.
Pension A regular amount of money paid to a person.
Postcode A code of letters and numbers used as part of a postal address to help in sorting of mail.
Profit The difference between what a business earns and what it spends in running costs.
Receipt A written acknowledgement by a person for receiving money or goods.
Recorded delivery A Post Office service where a record is kept of the posting and delivery of an item of mail.
Registered delivery Insuring an item against loss or damage in the mail.
Supervisor An overseer in charge of other workers.

Further Reading

Eldon, Kathy & Mike *Tom-tom to Television* (Wayland, 1977)
Howard, Sam *Communications Machines* (Blackwell/Raintree, 1980)
King, Charles *Modern Communications* (Harrap, 1970)
Page, Robert *The Story of the Post* (A & C Black, 1967)
Royston, Olive *The Post Office* (Routledge & Kegan Paul, 1972)
Barnes, Michael J. *Telecommunications* (Wayland, 1979)

Index

Administrators 8
Airmail 24, 25, 44–5
Automatic letter facer 12

British Telecom 8, 28, 52–3, 54
  56

Collection of mail 8, 12, 19, 24
Competition 10–11, 24, 27, 56
Contract Local Delivery Service
  25
Counter staff 8, 10–11, 23, 24

Definitive stamps 49
Delivery of mail 8, 10, 16–17,
  18–19
Department of Industry 28
Director of Design 47
Distribution of mail 12, 14, 18–19
  24–5, 38, 42–3, 44–5, 56
Dockwra, William 35

'Ernie' 27

First-class mail 10, 12, 29, 45
Flying Royal Mail Service 45

Great Train Robbery 40–41

Head postmaster 8
Head post office 23
'Heartbreak Corner' 24
Hill, Sir Rowland 35, 51
History of postal services 6, 18,
  30–31, 32–3, 34–5, 36–7, 42–3,
  44, 46, 48, 50–51

Letter bomb 4, 45
Letter-mail 8

Mailcoaches 34, 35
Mailtrains 35, 38–9, 40–41
Managers 23
Mechanics 8, 18
Mercury exchange 54
Microwaves 54
Monopoly 56

National Girobank 9, 27, 28
National Savings Bank 27
Nightrider system 25

Overseas mail office 45

Palmer, John 34
Parcel-mail 6, 8, 14, 24–5
Penny Black 46, 48, 51
Penny post 35
Postal cadet 22
Postal Marketing Department 46
Postal zones 24–5
Postman higher grade 22
Post Office Guide 24
Post Office Tower 54–5
Post Office Users National
  Council 28
Premium bonds 26–7

Recorded delivery 10, 19
Recruitment 22–3, 53
Registered mail 15, 19

Seamail 24, 45
Second-class mail 10, 12
Segregator 12
Sorting of mail 4, 8, 12–13, 14–15, 16, 39, 56
Special delivery 10
Stamp Advisory Committee 47, 48
Stamp Bug Club 50
Stamps
   collecting 49, 50–51
   designing 46–7
   production 48–9
Sub-post offices 8, 20–21
Subscriber Trunk Dialling (S.T.D.) 52
Supervisor 4, 5, 15, 16, 22

Technicians 8, 53
Telecommunications 28, 54–5, 56
Telegrams 11
Telephones 8, 11, 28, 29, 52
Telex 52–3, 54
Training 15, 21, 23
Travelling Post Offices 38–9
Trunk calls 29, 52

Underground railway 42–3
Uniforms 16

West German postal service 29
Witherings, Thomas 34

Acknowledgements

The author and the publishers would like to thank the following people for their help in producing this book: Mr G. Wilson, Postmaster at Boston; Mr R. Jewell, Postmaster at Nottingham; and Miss M. Edwards of the Public Relations Department of the Post Office in London.

The photographs in this book were taken by Chris Fairclough, except for the following: Post Office copyright reserved, pages 20, 32, 33, (top), 34, 35 (both), 37 (bottom), 38, 39, 42, 44, 46, 47, 49; Wayland Picture Library, pages 27, 31 (both), 33 (bottom), 36, 40–41, 43, 45 (both), 48, 51, 52, 53 (both), 54, 55 (both), 56, 57 (both).

The cover photograph was taken with equipment kindly lent by Nikon (UK) Ltd.